The Constitution of the
State of Vermont:
A Quick Reference Guide

Bootblack Budget Books
Copyright 2018 ©
ISBN-13: 978-1724580757
ISBN-10: 1724580752

Contents:

CHAPTER II: PLAN OR FRAME OF GOVERNMENT

DELEGATION AND DISTRIBUTION
OF POWERS – Page 22

Legislative Department – Page 23

6

EXECUTIVE DEPARTMENT – Page 29

JUDICIARY DEPARTMENT – Page 32

QUALIFICATIONS OF FREEMEN AND FREEWOMEN – Page 37

Article 42. Voter's Qualifications and Oath

OATH OF ALLEGIANCE; OATH OF OFFICE – Page 42

Article 56. Oaths of Allegiance and Office

IMPEACHMENT – Page 43

MILITIA – Page 44

Article 59. Militia

AMENDMENT OF THE CONSTITUTION – Page 49

15

TEMPORARY PROVISIONS – Page 51

CHAPTER I: A DECLARATION OF THE RIGHTS OF THE INHABITANTSOF THE STATE OF VERMONT

Article 1. All Persons Born Free; Their Natural Rights; Slavery Prohibited

That all persons are born equally free and independent, and have certain natural, inherent, and unalienable rights, amongst which are the enjoying and defending life and liberty, acquiring, possessing and protecting property, and pursuing and obtaining happiness and safety; therefore no person born in this country, or brought from over sea, ought to be holden by law, to serve any person as a servant, slave or apprentice, after arriving to the age of twenty-one years, unless bound by the person's own consent, after arriving to such age, or bound by law for the payment of debts, damages, fines, costs, or the like.

Article 2. Private Property Subject to Public Use; Owner to be Paid

That private property ought to be subservient to public uses when necessity requires it, nevertheless, whenever any person's property is taken for the use of the public, the owner ought to receive an equivalent in money.

Article 3. Freedom in Religion; Right and Duty of Religious Worship

That all persons have a natural and unalienable right, to worship Almighty God, according to the dictates of their own consciences and understandings, as in their opinion shall be regulated by the word of God; and that no person ought to, or of right can be compelled to attend any religious worship, or erect or support any place of worship, or maintain any minister, contrary to the dictates of conscience, nor can any person be justly deprived or abridged of any civil right as a citizen, on account of religious sentiments, or peculia[r] mode of religious worship; and that no authority can, or ought to be vested in, or assumed by, any power whatever, that shall in any case interfere with, or in any manner control the rights of conscience, in the free exercise of religious worship. Nevertheless, every sect or denomination of christians ought to observe the sabbath or Lord's day, and keep up some sort of religious worship, which to them shall seem most agreeable to the revealed will of God.

Article 4. Remedy at Law Secured to All

Every person within this state ought to find a certain remedy, by having recourse to the laws, for all injuries or wrongs which one may receive in person, property or character; every person ought to obtain right and justice, freely, and without being obliged to purchase it; completely and without any denial; promptly and without delay; comformably to the laws.

Article 5. Internal Police

That the people of this state by their legal representatives, have the sole, inherent, and exclusive right of governing and regulating the internal police of the same.

Article 6. Officers Servants of the People

That all power being originally inherent in and co[n]sequently derived from the people, therefore, all officers of government, whether legislative or executive, are their trustees and servants; and at all times, in a legal way, accountable to them.

Article 7. Government for the People; They May Change It

That government is, or ought to be, instituted for the common benefit, protection, and security of the people, nation, or community, and not for the particular emolument or advantage of any single person, family, or set of persons, who are a part only of that community; and that the community hath an indubitable, unalienable, and indefeasible right, to reform or alter government, in such manner as shall be, by that community, judged most conducive to the public weal.

Article 8. Elections to be Free and Pure; Rights of Voters Therein

That all elections ought to be free and without corruption, and that all voters, having a sufficient, evident, common interest with, and attachment to the community, have a right to elect officers, and be elected into office, agreeably to the regulations made in this constitution.

Article 9. Citizens Rights and Duties in the State; Bearing Arms; Taxation

That every member of society hath a right to be protected in the enjoyment of life, liberty, and property, and therefore is bound to contribute the member's proportion towards the expence of that protection, and yield personal service, when necessary, or an equivalent thereto, but no part of any person's property can be justly taken, or applied to public uses, without the person's own consent, or that of the Representative Body, nor can any person who is conscientiously scrupulous of bearing arms, be justly compelled thereto, if such person will pay such equivalent; nor are the people bound by any law but such as they have in like manner assented to, for their common good: and previous to any law being made to raise a tax, the purpose for which it is to be raised ought to appear evident to the Legislature to be of more service to community than the money would be if not collected.

Article 10. Rights of Persons Accused of Crime; Personal Liberty; Waiver o f Jury Trial

That in all prosecutions for criminal offenses, a person hath a right to be heard by oneself and by counsel; to demand the cause and nature of the accusation; to be confronted with the witnesses; to call for evidence in the person's favor, and a speedy public trial by an impartial jury of the country; without the unanimous consent of which jury, the person cannot be found guilty; nor can a person be compelled to give evidence against oneself; nor can any person be justly deprived of liberty, except by the laws of the land, or the judgment of the person's peers; provided, nevertheless, in criminal prosecutions for offenses not punishable by death, the accused, with the consent of the prosecuting officer entered of record, may in open court or by a writing signed by the accused and filed with the court, waive the right to a jury trial and submit the issue of the accused's guilt to the determination and judgment of the court without a jury.

Article 11. Search and Seizure Regulated

That the people have a right to hold themselves, their houses, papers, and possessions, free from search or seizure; and therefore warrants, without oath or affirmation first made, affording sufficient foundation for them, and whereby by any officer or messenger may be commanded or required to search suspected places, or to seize any person or persons, his, her or their property, not particularly described, are contrary to that right, and ought not to be granted.

Article 12. Trial by Jury to be Held Sacred

That when any issue in fact, proper for the cognizance of a jury is joined in a court of law, the parties have a right to trial by jury, which ought to be held sacred.

Article 13. Freedom of Speech and of the Press

That the people have a right to freedom of speech, and of writing and publishing their sentiments, concerning the transactions of government, and therefore the freedom of the press ought not to be restrained.

Article 14. Immunity for Words Spoken in Legislative Debate

The freedom of deliberation, speech, and debate, in the Legislature, is so essential to the rights of the people, that it cannot be the foundation of any accusation or prosecution, action or complaint, in any other court or place whatsoever.

Article 15. Legislature Only May Suspend Laws

The power of suspending laws, or the execution of laws, ought never to be exercised but by the Legislature, or by authority derived from it, to be exercised in such particular cases, as this constitution, or the Legislature shall provide for.

Article 16. Right to Bear Arms; Standing Armies; Military Power Subordinate to Civil

That the people have a right to bear arms for the defence of themselves and the State--and as standing armies in time of peace are dangerous to liberty, they ought not to be kept up; and that the military should be kept under strict subordination to and governed by the civil power.

Article 17. Martial Law Restricted

That no person in this state can in any case be subjected to law martial, or to any penalties or pains by virtue of that law except those employed in the army, and the militia in actual service.

Article 18. Regard to Fundamental Principles and Virtues Necessary to Preserve Liberty

That frequent recurrence to fundamental principles, and a firm adherence to justice, moderation, temperance, industry, and frugality, are absolutely necessary to preserve the blessings of liberty, and keep government free; the people ought, therefore to pay particular attention to these points, in the choice of officers and representatives, and have a right, in a legal way, to exact a due and constant regard to them, from their legislators and magistrates, in making and executing such laws as are necessary for the good government of the State.

Article 19. Right to Emigrate

That all people have a natural and inherent right to emigrate from one state to another that will receive them.

Article 20. Right to Assemble, Instruct and Petition

That the people have a right to assemble together to consult for their common good--to instruct their Representatives--and to apply to the Legislature for redress of grievances, by address, petition or remonstrance.

Article 21. No Transportation for Trial

That no person shall be liable to be transported out of this state for trial for any offence committed within the same.

CHAPTER II: PLAN OR FRAME OF GOVERNMENT

DELEGATION AND DISTRIBUTION OF POWERS

Article 1. Governing Power

The Commonwealth or State of Vermont shall be governed by a Governor (or Lieutenant-Governor), a Senate and a House of Representatives, in manner and form following:

Article 2. Supreme Legislative Power

The Supreme Legislative power shall be exercised by a Senate and a House of Representatives.

Article 3. Supreme Executive Power

The Supreme Executive power shall be exercised by a Governor, or in the Governor's absence, a Lieutenant-Governor.

Article 4. Judiciary

The judicial power of the State shall be vested in a unified judicial system which shall be composed of a Supreme Court, a Superior Court, and such other subordinate courts as the General Assembly may from time to time ordain and establish.

Article 5. Departments to be Distinct

The Legislative, Executive, and Judiciary departments, shall be separate and distinct, so that neither exercise the powers properly belonging to the others.

Legislative Department

Article 6. Legislative Powers

The Senate and the House of Representatives shall be styled, The General Assembly of the State of Vermont . Each shall have and exercise the like powers in all acts of legislation; and no bill, resolution, or other thing, which shall have been passed by the one, shall have the effect of, or be declared to be, a law, without the concurrence of the other. Provided, That all Revenue bills shall originate in the House of Representatives; but the Senate may propose or concur in amendments, as on other bills. Neither House during the session of the General Assembly, shall, without the consent of the other, adjourn for more than three days, nor to any other place than that in which the two Houses shall be sitting; and in case of disagreement between the two Houses with respect to adjournment, the Governor may adjourn them to such time as the Governor shall think proper. They may prepare bills and enact them into laws, redress grievances, grant charters of incorporation, subject to the provisions of section 69, constitute towns, borroughs, cities and counties; and they shall have all other powers necessary for the Legislature of a free and sovereign State; but they shall have no power to add to, alter, abolish, or infringe any part of this Constitution.

Article 7. Biennial Sessions

The General Assembly shall meet biennially on the first Wednesday next after the first Monday of January, beginning in A.D. 1915.

Article 8. Doors of General Assembly to be Open

The doors of the House in which the General Assembly of this Commonwealth shall sit, shall be open for the admission of all persons who behave decently, except only when the welfare of the State may require them to be shut.

Article 9. Journals; Yeas and Nays

The votes and proceedings of the General Assembly shall be printed (when one-third of the members of either House think It necessary) as soon as convenient after the end of the session, with the yeas and nays of the House of Representatives on any question when required by five members, and of the Senate when required by one Senator, (except where the votes shall be taken by ballot), in which case every member of either House shall have a right to insert the reasons of the member's vote upon the minutes.

Article 10. Style of Laws

This style of the laws of this State shall be, It is hereby enacted by the General Assembly of the State of Vermont .

Article 11. Governor to Approve Bills; Veto
Proceedings Thereon; Non-action

Every bill which shall have passed the Senate and House of Representatives shall, before it becomes a law, be presented to the Governor; if the Governor approve, the Governor shall sign it; if not, the Governor shall return it, with objections in writing, to the House in which it shall have originated; which shall proceed to reconsider it. If, upon such reconsideration, two-thirds of the members present of that House shall pass the bill, it shall, together with the objections, be sent to the other House, by which it shall likewise be reconsidered, and if approved by two-thirds of the members present of that House, it shall become a law.

But, in all such cases, the votes of both Houses shall be taken by yeas and nays, and the names of the persons voting for or against the bill shall be entered on the journal of each House, respectively. If any bill shall not be returned by the Governor, as aforesaid, within five days (Sundays excepted) after it shall have been presented to the Governor, the same shall become a law in like manner as if the Governor had signed it; unless the two Houses by their adjournment, within three days after the presentation of such bill shall prevent its return; in which case it shall not become a law.

Article 12. Fees for Advocating Bills, Etc.

No member of the General Assembly shall, directly or indirectly, receive any fee or reward, to bring forward or advocate any bill, petition, or other business to be transacted in the Legislature; or advocate any cause, as counsel in either House of legislation, except when employed in behalf of the State.

Article 13. Representatives; Number

The House of Representatives shall be composed of one hundred fifty Representatives. The voters of each representative district established by law shall elect one or two Representatives from that district, the number from each district to be established by the General Assembly.

In establishing representative districts, which shall afford equality of representation, the General Assembly shall seek to maintain geographical compactness and contiguity and to adhere to boundaries of counties and other existing political subdivisions.

Article 14. Powers of House

The Representatives so chosen (a majority of whom shall constitute a quorum for transacting any other business than raising a State tax, for which two-thirds of the members elected shall be present) shall meet as required by section 7, and shall be styled the House of Representatives: they shall have power to choose their Speaker, their Clerk and other necessary officers, sit on their own adjournment subject to the limitations of section 6, judge of the elections and qualifications of their own members; they may expel members, but not for causes known to their constituents antecedent to their election, administer oaths and affirmations in matters depending before them, and impeach state criminals.

Article 15. Residence of Representatives and Senators

No person shall be elected a Representative or a Senator until the person has resided in this State two years, the last year of which shall be in the legislative district for which the person is elected.

Article 16. Representatives Oaths

The Representatives having met, and chosen their Speaker and Clerk, shall each of them, before they proceed to business, take and subscribe, as well the oath or affirmation of allegiance hereinafter directed (except where they shall produce certificates of their having theretofore taken and subscribed the same) as the following oath or affirmation:

You do solemnly swear (or affirm) that as a member of this Assembly, you will not propose, or assent to, any bill, vote or resolution, which shall appear to you injurious to the people, nor do nor consent to any act or thing whatever, that shall have a tendency to lessen or abridge their rights and privileges, as declared by the Constitution of this State; but will, in all things, conduct yourself as a faithful, honest Representative and guardian of the people, according to the best of your judgment and ability.

Under the pains and penalties of perjury.

Article 17. Oath of Senators and Representatives

The Representatives having met on the day appointed by law for the commencement of a biennial session of the General Assembly, and chosen their Speaker, and the Senators having met, shall, before they proceed to business, take and subscribe the following oath, in addition to the oath prescribed in the foregoing section:

You do solemnly swear (or affirm) that you did not at the time of your election to this body, and that you do not now, hold any office of profit or trust under the authority of Congress. So help you God. (Or in the case of an affirmation) Under the pains and penalties of perjury. The words "office of profit or trust under the authority of Congress" shall be construed to mean any office created directly or indirectly by Congress, and for which emolument is provided from the Treasury of the United States, other than that of a member of the commissioned or enlisted personnel in the reserve components of the armed forces of the United States while not on extended active duty.

Article 18. Senators; Numbers; Qualifications

The Senate shall be composed of thirty Senators to be of the senatorial district from which they are elected. The voters of each senatorial district established by law shall elect one or more Senators from that district, the number from each district to be established by the General Assembly.

In establishing senatorial districts, which shall afford equality of representation, the General Assembly shall seek to maintain geographical compactness and contiguity and to adhere to boundaries of counties and other existing political subdivisions.

Article 19. Powers of Senate; Lieutenant-Governor's Duties

The Senate shall have the like powers to decide on the election and qualifications of, and to expel any of, its members, make its own rules, and appoint its own officers, as are incident to, or are possessed by, the House of Representatives. A majority shall constitute a quorum. The Lieutenant-Governor shall be President of the Senate, except when exercising the office of Governor, or when the office of the Lieutenant-Governor shall be vacant, or in the absence of the Lieutenant-Governor, in which cases the Senate shall appoint one of its own members to be President of the Senate, pro tempore . And the President of the Senate shall have a casting vote, but no other.

EXECUTIVE DEPARTMENT

Article 20. Governor; Executive Power

The Governor, and in the Governor's absence, the Lieutenant-Governor, shall have power to commission all officers, and also to appoint officers, except where provision is, or shall be, otherwise made by law or this Frame of Government; and shall supply every vacancy in any office, occasioned by death or otherwise, until the office can be filled in the manner directed by law or this Constitution. The Governor is to correspond with other States, transact business with officers of government, civil and military, and prepare such business as may appear necessary, to lay before the General Assembly. The Governor shall have power to grant pardons and remit fines in all cases whatsoever, except in treason in which the Governor shall have power to grant reprieves, but not to pardon, until after the end of the next session of the General Assembly; and except in cases of impeachment, in which the Governor shall not grant reprieve or pardon, and there shall be no remission, or mitigation of punishment, but by act of legislation. The Governor is also to take care that the laws be faithfully executed. The Governor is to expedite the execution of such measures as may be resolved upon by the General Assembly. And the Governor may draw upon the Treasury for such sums as may be appropriated by the General Assembly. The Governor may also lay embargoes, or prohibit the exportation of any commodity, for any time not exceeding thirty days, in the recess of the General Assembly only. The Governor may grant such licenses as shall be directed by law; and shall have power to call together the General Assembly, when necessary, before the day to which they shall stand adjourned. The Governor shall be Captain-General and Commander-in-Chief of the forces of the State, but shall not command in person, in time of war, or insurrection, unless by the advice and consent of the Senate, and no longer than they shall approve thereof. And the Lieutenant-Governor shall, by virtue of office, be Lieutenant-General of all the forces of the State.

Article 21. Secretary of Civil and Military Affairs

The Governor may have a Secretary of Civil and Military Affairs, to be appointed during pleasure, whose services the Governor may at all times command; and for whose compensation provisions shall be made by law.

Article 22. Commissions; State Seal

All commissions shall be in the name of The People of the State of Vermont , sealed with the State Seal, signed by the Governor, and in the absence of the Governor by the Lieutenant-Governor, and attested by the Secretary; which Seal shall be kept by the Governor.

Article 23. Residence Of Governor And Lieutenant-Governor

No person shall be eligible to the office of Governor or Lieutenant-Governor until the person shall have resided in this State four years next preceding the day of election.

Article 24. Vacancy in Office of Governor, Lieutenant-Governor and Treasurer

The Legislature shall provide by general law what officer shall act as Governor whenever there shall be a vacancy in both the offices of Governor and Lieutenant-Governor, occasioned by a failure to elect, or by the removal from office, or by the death or resignation of both Governor and Lieutenant-Governor, or by the inability of both Governor and Lieutenant-Governor to exercise the powers and discharge the duties of the office of Governor; and such officer so designated, shall exercise the powers and discharge the duties appertaining to the office of Governor accordingly until the disability shall be removed, or a Governor shall be elected. And in case there shall be a vacancy in the office of Treasurer, by reason of any of the causes enumerated, the Governor shall appoint a Treasurer for the time being, who shall act as Treasurer until the disability shall be removed, or a new election shall be made.

Article 25. Security Given by Treasurer and Sheriffs

The Treasurer of the State shall, before entering upon the duties of office, give sufficient security to the Secretary of State, in behalf of the State of Vermont, before the Governor of the State or one of the Justices of the Supreme Court. And Sheriffs, before entering upon the duties of their offices, shall give sufficient security in such manner and in such sums as shall be directed by the Legislature.

Article 26. Treasurer's Accounts

The Treasurer's accounts shall be annually audited, and a fair state thereof laid before the General Assembly at its biennial session in January.

Article 27. Drawing Money From Treasury

No money shall be drawn out of the Treasury, unless first appropriated by act of legislation.

JUDICIARY DEPARTMENT

Article 28. Courts of Justice

The Courts of Justice shall be open for the trial of all causes proper for their cognizance; and justice shall be therein impartially administered, without corruption or unnecessary delay.

Article 29. The Supreme Court; Composition

The Supreme Court shall consist of the Chief Justice of the State and four associate justices of the Supreme Court.

Article 30. Supreme Court; Jurisdiction

The Supreme Court shall exercise appellate jurisdiction in all cases, criminal and civil, under such terms and conditions as it shall specify in rules not inconsistent with law. The Supreme Court shall have original jurisdiction only as provided by law, but it shall have the power to issue all writs necessary or appropriate in aid of its appellate jurisdiction. The Supreme Court shall have administrative control of all the courts of the state, and disciplinary authority concerning all judicial officers and attorneys at law in the State.

Article 31. Lower Courts; Jurisdiction

All other courts of this State shall have original and appellate jurisdiction as provided by law. All courts except the Supreme Court may be divided into geographical and functional divisions as provided by law or by judicial rules adopted by the Supreme Court not inconsistent with law. The jurisdiction of geographical and functional divisions shall be as provided by law or by judicial rules not inconsistent with law. The courts of this state may exercise equity jurisdiction as well as law jurisdiction in civil proceedings as may be provided by law or by judicial rules not inconsistent with law.

Article 32. Filling Judicial Vacancies

The Governor, with the advice and consent of the Senate, shall fill a vacancy in the office of the Chief Justice of the State, associate justice of the Supreme Court or judge of any other court, except the office of Assistant Judge and of Judge of Probate, from a list of nominees presented by a judicial nominating body established by the General Assembly having authority to apply reasonable standards of selection.

Article 33. Interim Judicial Appointments

When the Senate is not in session, the Governor may make an interim appointment to fill a vacancy in the office of chief justice, associate justice of the Supreme Court or judge of any other court, except the office of Assistant Judge and of Judge of Probate, from a list of nominees presented by the judicial nominating body. A justice or judge so appointed shall hold office, with all the powers incident to the office, until the Senate convenes and acts upon the appointment submitted by the Governor. Thereafter, the appointee shall continue in office if the Senate consents to the appointment. If the appointment is not confirmed upon vote of the Senate, the appointment shall be terminated and a vacancy in the office will be created.

Article 34. Judicial Term of Office

The justices of the Supreme Court and judges of all subordinate courts, except Assistant Judges and Judges of Probate, shall hold office for terms of six years except when holding office under an interim appointment. At the end of the initial six year term and at the end of each six year term thereafter, such justice or judge may give notice in the manner provided by law of a desire to continue in office. When such justice or judge gives the required notice, the question of continuance in office shall be submitted to the General Assembly and the justice or judge shall continue in office for another term of six years unless a majority of the members of the General Assembly voting on the question vote against continuation in office.

Article 35. Mandatory Retirement

All justices of the Supreme Court and judges of all subordinate courts shall be retired at such age, not less than seventy years of age, as the General Assembly may prescribe by law, or, if the General Assembly has not so provided by law, at the end of the calendar year in which they attain seventy years of age or at the end of the term of election during which they attain seventy years of age, as the case may be, and shall be pensioned as provided by law. The chief justice may from time to time appoint retired justices and judges to special assignments as permitted under the rules of the Supreme Court.

Article 36. Suspension and Removal; Implementation Procedures for Sections 32 Through 36

The justices of the Supreme Court and the judges of all subordinate courts shall hold office during good behavior for the terms for which they are appointed. The Supreme Court in the exercise of its disciplinary power over the judiciary of the state may suspend justices of the Supreme Court and judges of all subordinate courts from the judicial function for such cause and in such manner as may be provided by law. The General Assembly may establish procedures for the implementation of the provisions of sections thirty-two through thirty-six.

Article 37. Rule-Making Power

The Supreme Court shall make and promulgate rules governing the administration of all courts, and shall make and promulgate rules governing practice and procedure in civil and criminal cases in all courts. Any rule adopted by the Supreme Court may be revised by the General Assembly.

Article 38. Jury Trials

Trials of issues, proper for the cognizance of a Jury as established by law or by judicial rules adopted by the Supreme Court not inconsistent with law, in the Supreme Court, the Superior Court and other subordinate courts, shall be by Jury, except where parties otherwise agree; and great care ought to be taken to prevent corruption or partiality in the choice and return, or appointment of Juries.

Article 39. Forms of Prosecutions and Indictments; Fines

All prosecutions shall commence, By the authority of the State of Vermont . All Indictments shall conclude with these words, against the peace and dignity of the State . And all fines shall be proportioned to the offences.

Article 40. Excessive Bail Prohibited; Prisoners Bailable; Imprisonment for Debt Prohibited

Excessive bail shall not be exacted for bailable offenses. All persons shall be bailable by sufficient sureties, except as follows:

(1) A person accused of an offense punishable by death or life imprisonment may be held without bail when the evidence of guilt is great.

(2) A person accused of a felony, an element of which involves an act of violence against another person, may be held without bail when the evidence of guilt is great and the court finds, based upon clear and convincing evidence, that the person's release poses a substantial threat of physical violence to any person and that no condition or combination of conditions of release will reasonably prevent the physical violence. A person held without bail prior to trial under this paragraph shall be entitled to review de novo by a single justice of the Supreme Court forthwith.

(3) A person awaiting sentence, or sentenced pending appeal, may be held without bail for any offense.

A person held without bail prior to trial shall be entitled to review of that determination by a panel of three Supreme Court Justices within seven days after bail is denied.

Except in the case of an offense punishable by death or life imprisonment, if a person is held without bail prior to trial, the trial of the person shall be commenced not more than 60 days after bail is denied. If the trial is not commenced within 60 days and the delay is not attributable to the defense, the court shall immediately schedule a bail hearing and shall set bail for the person.

No person shall be imprisoned for debt.

Article 41. Habeas Corpus

The Writ of Habeas Corpus shall in no case be suspended. It shall be a writ issuable of right; and the General Assembly shall make provision to render it a speedy and effectual remedy in all cases proper therefor.

QUALIFICATIONS OF FREEMEN AND FREEWOMEN

Article 42. Voter's Qualifications and Oath

Every person of the full age of eighteen years who is a citizen of the United States, having resided in this State for the period established by the General Assembly and who is of a quiet and peaceable behavior, and will take the following oath or affirmation, shall be entitled to all the privileges of a voter of this state:

You solemnly swear (or affirm) that whenever you give your vote or suffrage, touching any matter that concerns the State of Vermont, you will do it so as in your conscience you shall judge will most conduce to the best good of the same, as established by the Constitution, without fear or favor of any person.
Every person who will attain the full age of eighteen years by the date of the general election who is a citizen of the United States, having resided in this State for the period established by the General Assembly and who is of a quiet and peaceable behavior, and will take the oath or affirmation set forth in this section, shall be entitled to vote in the primary election.

ELECTIONS; OFFICERS; TERMS OF OFFICE

Article 43. Biennial Elections

The Governor, Lieutenant-Governor, Treasurer, Secretary of State, Auditor of Accounts, Senators, Town Representatives, Assistant Judges of the County Court, Sheriffs, High Bailiffs, State's Attorneys, Judges of Probate and Justices of the Peace, shall be elected biennially on the first Tuesday next after the first Monday of November, beginning in A.D. 1914.

Article 44. Election of Representatives and Senators

Senators and Representatives shall be elected to office at a general election to be held biennially on the first Tuesday next after the first Monday of November, A.D. 1974.

Article 45. Manner of Election

The manner of election, certification, and filling of vacancies in office of Senators and Representatives shall be as established by law.

Article 46. Terms of Senators and Representatives

The term of office of Senators and Representatives shall be two years, commencing on the first Wednesday next after the first Monday of January following their election.

Article 47. Election of Governor, Lieutenant-Governor and Treasurer

The voters of each town shall, on the day of election for choosing Representatives to attend the General Assembly, bring in their votes for Governor, with the name fairly written, to the Constable, who shall seal them up, and write on them, Votes for Governor, and deliver them to the Representatives chosen to attend the General Assembly; and at the opening of the General

Assembly, there shall be a committee appointed out of the Senate and House of Representatives, who, after being duly sworn to the faithful discharge of their trust, shall proceed to receive, sort, and count the votes for Governor, and declare the person who has the major part of the votes, to be Governor for the two years ensuing. The Lieutenant-Governor and the Treasurer shall be chosen in the manner above directed. The votes for Governor, Lieutenant-Governor, and Treasurer, of the State, shall be sorted and counted, and the result declared, by a committee appointed by the Senate and House of Representatives.

If, at any time, there shall be no election, of Governor, Lieutenant-Governor, or Treasurer, of the State, the Senate and House of Representatives shall by a joint ballot, elect to fill the office, not filled as aforesaid, one of the three candidates for such office (if there be so many) for whom the greatest number of votes shall have been returned.

Article 48. Election of Secretary of State and Auditor of Accounts

The Secretary of State and the Auditor of Accounts shall be elected by the voters of the State upon the same ticket with the Governor, Lieutenant-Governor and Treasurer; and the Legislature shall carry this provision into effect by appropriate legislation.

Article 49. Term of Governor, Lieutenant-Governor and Treasurer

The term of office of the Governor, Lieutenant-Governor and Treasurer of the State, respectively, shall commence when they shall be chosen and qualified, and shall continue for the term of two years, or until their successors shall be chosen and qualified, or to the adjournment of the session of the Legislature at which, by the Constitution and laws, their successors are required to be chosen, and not after such adjournment.

Article 50. Election of Assistant Judges, Sheriffs and State's Attorneys

The Assistant Judges shall be elected by the voters of their respective districts as established by law. Their judicial functions shall be established by law. Their term of office shall be four years and shall commence on the first day of February next after their election.
Sheriffs shall be elected by the voters of their respective districts as established by law. Their term of office shall be four years and shall commence on the first day of February next after their election.

State's Attorneys shall be elected by the voters of their respective districts as established by law. Their term of office shall be four years and shall commence on the first day of February next after their election.

Article 51. Election of Judges of Probate

Judges of Probate shall be elected by the voters of their respective districts as established by law. The General Assembly may establish by law qualifications for the election to and holding of such office. Their term of office shall be four years and shall commence on the first day of February next after their election.

Article 52. Election of Justices of the Peace; Apportionment

Justices of the Peace shall be elected by the voters of their respective towns; and towns having less than one thousand inhabitants may elect any number of Justices of the Peace not exceeding five; towns having one thousand and less than two thousand inhabitants, may elect seven; towns having two thousand and less than three thousand inhabitants, may elect ten; towns having three thousand and less than five thousand inhabitants, may elect twelve; and towns having five thousand, or more, inhabitants, may elect fifteen Justices of the Peace. Justices of the Peace shall not exercise judicial powers, except that they may serve as magistrates when so commissioned by the Supreme Court.

Article 53. Election of Assistant Judges, Sheriffs, State's Attorneys, Judges of Probate, and Justices of the Peace

The manner and certification of election and filling of vacancies in the offices of Assistant Judges, Sheriffs, State's Attorneys, Judges of Probate and Justices of the Peace shall be as established by law.

Article 54. Incompatible Offices

No person in this State shall be capable of holding or exercising more than one of the following offices at the same time: Governor, Lieutenant-Governor, Justice of the Supreme Court, Treasurer of the State, member of the Senate, member of the House of Representatives, Surveyor-General, or Sheriff. Nor shall any person holding any office of profit or trust under the authority of Congress, other than a member of the commissioned or enlisted personnel in the reserve components of the armed forces of the United States while not on extended active duty, be eligible to any appointment in the Legislature, or to any executive or judiciary office under this State.

Article 55. Freedom of Elections; Bribery

All elections, whether by the people or the Legislature, shall be free and voluntary: and any elector who shall receive any gift or reward for the elector's vote, in meat, drink, moneys or otherwise, shall forfeit the right to elect at that time, and suffer such other penalty as the law shall direct; and any person who shall directly or indirectly give, promise, or bestow, any such rewards to be elected, shall thereby be rendered incapable to serve for the ensuing year, and be subject to such further punishment as the Legislature shall direct.

OATH OF ALLEGIANCE; OATH OF OFFICE

Article 56. Oaths of Allegiance and Office

Every officer, whether judicial, executive, or military, in authority under this State, before entering upon the execution of office, shall take and subscribe the following oath or affirmation of allegiance to this State, (unless the officer shall produce evidence that the officer has before taken the same) and also the following oath or affirmation of office, except military officers, and such as shall be exempted by the Legislature.

The Oath or Affirmation of Allegiance

You _____ do solemnly swear (or affirm) that you will be true and faithful to the State of Vermont, and that you will not, directly or indirectly, do any act or thing injurious to the Constitution or Government thereof . (If an oath) So help you God . (If an affirmation) Under the pains and penalties of perjury

.

The Oath or Affirmation of Office

You _____ do solemnly swear (or affirm) that you will faithfully execute the office of _____ for the _____ of _____ and will therein do equal right and justice to all persons, to the best of your judgment and ability, according to law . (If an oath) So help you God . (If an affirmation) Under the pains and penalties of perjury .

IMPEACHMENT

Article 57. Impeachments, House May Order

The House of Representatives shall have the power to order impeachments, which shall in all cases be by a vote of two-thirds of its members.

Article 58. Liability To; Senate To Try; Judgment

Every officer of State, whether judicial or executive, shall be liable to be impeached by the House of Representatives, either when in office or after resignation or removal for maladministration.

The Senate shall have the sole power of trying and deciding upon all impeachments. When sitting for that purpose, they shall be on oath, or affirmation, and no person shall be convicted, without the concurrence of two-thirds of the members present. Judgment in cases of impeachment shall not extend further than to removal from office and disqualification to hold or enjoy any office of honor, or profit, or trust, under this State. But the person convicted shall, nevertheless, be liable and subject to indictment, trial, judgment, and punishment, according to law.

MILITIA

Article 59. Militia

The inhabitants of this State shall be trained and armed for its defense, under such regulations, restrictions, and exceptions, as Congress, agreeably to the Constitution of the United States, and the Legislature of this State, shall direct.

GENERAL PROVISIONS

Article 60. Legislature Restricted

No person ought in any case, or in any time, to be declared guilty of treason or felony, by the Legislature, nor to have a sentence upon conviction for felony commuted, remitted, or mitigated by the Legislature.

Article 61. Offices of Profit; Compensation; Illegal Fees ·

As all persons of full age, to preserve their independence (if without a sufficient estate) ought to have some profession, calling, trade, or farm, whereby they may honestly subsist, there can be no necessity for, nor use in, establishing offices of profit, the usual effects of which are dependence and servility, unbecoming free citizens, in the possessors or expectants, and faction, contention and discord among the people. But if any person is called into public service to the prejudice of that person's private affairs, the person has a right to a reasonable compensation; and whenever an office through increase of fees or otherwise, becomes so profitable as to occasion many to apply for it, the profit ought to be lessened by the Legislature. And if any officer shall wittingly and wilfully, take greater fees than the law allows, it shall ever after disqualify that person from holding any office in this State until the person shall be restored by act of legislation.

Article 62. Record of Deeds

All deeds and conveyances of lands shall be recorded in the Town Clerk's office in their respective towns; and, for want thereof, in the County Clerk's office in the same county.

Article 63. Entails to be Regulated

The Legislature shall regulate entails in such manner as to prevent perpetuities.

Article 64. Punishment at Hard Labor, When

To deter more effectually from the commission of crimes, by continued visible punishments of long duration, and to make sanguinary punishments less necessary, means ought to be provided for punishing by hard labor, those who shall be convicted of crimes not capital, whereby the criminal shall be employed for the benefit of the public, or for the reparation of injuries done to private persons: and all persons at proper times ought to be permitted to see them at their labor.

Article 65. Suicide's Estate not Forfeited; No Deodand

The estates of such persons as may destroy their own lives, shall not, for that offence, be forfeited, but shall descend or ascend in the same manner as if such persons had died in a natural way. Nor shall any article which shall accidentally occasion the death of any person, be deemed a deodand, or in any wise forfeited on account of such misfortune.

Article 66. Citizenship

Every person of good character, who comes to settle in this State, having first taken an oath or affirmation of allegiance to the same, may purchase, or by other just means acquire, hold and transfer land or other real estate; and after one year's residence shall be deemed a free denizen thereof, and entitled to all rights of a natural born subject of this State, except those privileges, the right to which is herein elsewhere determined, and except also that such person shall not be capable of being elected Treasurer, or Representative in Assembly, until after two years' residence, nor be eligible to the office of Governor or Lieutenant-Governor until the person shall have resided in this State as required by section 23 of this Constitution.

Article 67. Hunting; Fowling and Fishing

The inhabitants of this State shall have liberty in seasonable times, to hunt and fowl on the lands they hold, and on other lands not inclosed, and in like manner to fish in all boatable and other waters (not private property) under proper regulations, to be made and provided by the General Assembly.

Article 68. Laws to Encourage Virtue and Prevent Vice; Schools; Religious Activities

Laws for the encouragement of virtue and prevention of vice and immorality ought to be constantly kept in force, and duly executed; and a competent number of schools ought to be maintained in each town unless the general assembly permits other provisions for the convenient instruction of youth. All religious societies, or bodies of people that may be united or incorporated for the advancement of religion and learning, or for other pious and charitable purposes, shall be encouraged and protected in the enjoyment of the privileges, immunities, and estates, which they in justice ought to enjoy, under such regulations as the general assembly of this state shall direct.

Article 69. Charters, Limit on Right to Grant

No charter of incorporation shall be granted, extended, changed or amended by special law, except for such municipal, charitable, educational, penal or reformatory corporations as are to be and remain under the patronage or control of the State; but the General Assembly shall provide by general laws for the organization of all corporations hereafter to be created. All general laws passed pursuant to this section may be altered from time to time or repealed.

Article 70. Workers Compensation

The General Assembly may pass laws compelling compensation for injuries received by employees in the course of their employment resulting in death or bodily hurt, for the benefit of such employees, their widows, widowers or next of kin. It may designate the class or classes of employers and employees to which such laws shall apply.

Article 71. Declaration of Rights not to be Violated

The Declaration of the political Rights and privileges of the inhabitants of this State, is hereby declared to be part of the Constitution of this Commonwealth; and ought not to be violated on any pretence whatsoever.

AMENDMENT OF THE CONSTITUTION

Article 72. Amending Constitution

At the biennial session of the General Assembly of this State which convenes in A.D. 1975, and at the biennial session convening every fourth year thereafter, the Senate by a vote of two-thirds of its members, may propose amendments to this Constitution, with the concurrence of a majority of the members of the House of Representatives with the amendment as proposed by the Senate. A proposed amendment so adopted by the Senate and concurred in by the House of Representatives shall be referred to the next biennial session of the General Assembly; and if at that last session a majority of the members of the Senate and a majority of the House of Representatives concur in the proposed amendment, it shall be the duty of the General Assembly to submit the proposal directly to the voters of the state. Any proposed amendment submitted to the voters of the state in accordance with this section which is approved by a majority of the voters voting thereon shall become part of the Constitution of this State.

Prior to the submission of a proposed amendment to a vote in accordance with this section, public notice of the proposed amendment shall be given by proclamation of the Governor. The General Assembly shall provide for the manner of voting on amendments proposed under this section, and shall enact legislation to carry the provisions of this section into effect.

Article 73. Manner of Apportionment of the General Assembly

The General Assembly shall establish senatorial districts within and including all of the state, and shall further establish representative districts within and including all of the state. At the biennial session following the taking of each decennial census under the authority of Congress, and at such other times as the General Assembly finds necessary, it shall revise the boundaries of the legislative districts and shall make a new apportionment of its membership in order to maintain equality of representation among the respective districts as nearly as is practicable. The General Assembly may provide for establishment of a legislative apportionment board to advise and assist the General Assembly concerning legislative apportionment. If the General Assembly fails to revise the legislative districts as required in this section, the Supreme Court in appropriate legal proceedings brought for that purpose may order reapportionment of the districts.

TEMPORARY PROVISIONS

Article 74. Extension of Terms of Certain Officers

The persons severally elected in 1912 to the offices mentioned in section 43 shall hold such offices until the term of their successors elected the first Tuesday next after the first Monday of November, A.D. 1914, shall begin as herein provided.

Article 75. Revision of Chapter II

The Justices of the Supreme Court are hereby authorized and directed to revise Chapter II of the Constitution by incorporating into said Chapter all amendments of the Constitution that are now or may be then in force and excluding therefrom all sections, clauses and words not in force and rearranged and renumbering the sections thereof under appropriate titles as in their judgment may be most logical and convenient; and said revised Chapter II as certified to the Secretary of State by said Justices or a majority thereof shall be a part of the Constitution of this State in substitution for existing Chapter II and all amendments thereof.

Article 76. Inclusive Language Revision

The Justices of the Supreme Court are hereby authorized and directed to revise Chapters I and II of the Constitution in gender inclusive language. This revision shall not alter the sense, meaning or effect of the sections of the Constitution. When the revision is certified by the Justices or a majority thereof to the Secretary of State, it shall be a substitute for existing Chapters I and II of the Constitution.